100 GAMES TO PLAY WITH A STICK

AUTHOR UNKNOWN

100 GAMES TO PLAY WITH A STICK

AUTHOR UNKNOWN

DSS Games
Santa Monica, California

www.dssgames.com

Illustrations by Ruth Palmer
Book design by Katie Burk

ISBN 978-1-7368682-0-1

First DSS GAMES Edition: June 2021
10 9 8 7 6 5 4 3 2 1

About This Book

The 100 stick games that follow were originally
published in the early 1950s. Author unknown.

Table of Contents

1. Stick in the Mud
Sticks + Mud = Fun

1. Go find some sticks.

2. Now go out back to that big mudhole.

3. Put 2 sticks in the mud.

4. The first stick that disappears in the mud is
   the winner or the loser.

5. You decide.

2. Walking Stick
Who can walk the farthest?

1. All players find a stick that is straight and sturdy.

2. This is now your walking stick.

3. Who can walk the farthest with their walking stick?

4. This is the game.

5. You may laugh and say, "Why do I need a walking stick?"

6. I am young and agile, and I have all my own teeth.

7. Just wait.

3. Capture the Stick
A twist on the old classic

1. Go find 2 sticks.

2. Set up 2 sticks on opposing sides of a field.

3. Each team's job is to capture the opposing team's stick by *any* means necessary.

4. This may get violent.

5. That's just part of the game.

4. Captain Stick
Captain's orders

1. Ahoy! Captain Stick here.

2. While you're aboard this ship, I need you to
   be the best seamen these seas have ever seen.

3. Now scrub the poop deck. I'm going to sleep
   in the captain's quarters.

4. First one to get scurvy wins a doubloon.

5. Now let's set sail.

5. Hide-and-Go-Stick
A twist on the old classic

1. Go find a stick.

2. Hide it somewhere.

3. Go try to find it.

4. If you find a stick, it might be the stick you hid
   or a different stick.

5. Are you sure this is the stick you hid?

6. Many sticks look alike.

6. Stick Shift
Off we go!

1. Go find a stick.

2. Sit in a chair and pretend you're driving a car.
   The stick is your stick shift.

3. A circular loaf of bread can be your
   steering wheel.

4. Your gas and brake pedals can be made from
   piles of dirt.

5. Drive anywhere you want.

7. Sticky Situation
Your perfect scapegoat

1. Go find a stick.

2. Do something your parents say not to do.

3. This could include beating up a drifter, playing
   with Daddy's Colt 45, or setting the shed on fire.

4. Did your parents find out?

5. Blame the stick.

8. Dr. Stick
My oh-so-important friend

1. Go find a stick that is self-centered.

2. Hello, Dr. Stick.

3. What wonderful things have you done for us today, Dr. Stick?

4. Did you save the little boy from polio?

5. Or remove the brain tumor from Father's head?

6. Where would we be without you, Dr. Stick?

7. How can we ever possibly thank you enough?

9. Slick Stick
Slippery

1. Go find a stick.

2. On the smooth side of the stick, put something slippery, like soap, motor oil, or lard.

3. See if you can hold on to the stick.

4. It will be hard because it's slippery.

10. Bad Stick
Has your stick committed tax fraud?

1. Go find a stick.

2. First you need to find out if your stick
   has done anything bad.

3. Has your stick been loitering, killed someone,
   or committed tax fraud?

4. If yes, then your stick needs to be punished.

5. You could forgive your stick, but then it will
   never learn its lesson and will live its whole life
   in squalor.

11. Stickmate
A twist on the old classic

1. Go find 32 sticks.

2. Assign different movement patterns to different groups of sticks.

3. Draw a checkerboard in the dirt.

4. When you have eliminated the other pieces and cornered the king stick, say "stickmate."

5. This game is very similar to chess.

12. Stick Casino
The house always wins

1. Go find some sticks.

2. Now find a treehouse, tent, or shed that would be suitable for your casino.

3. Invite all your friends—tell them to bring their best sticks.

4. Get them to risk all their sticks on frivolous games, and set the odds so you always win.

5. Play continues until your friends are broke.

13. Sticks Away!
A bombing game in which you annihilate the enemy

1. Go find a bunch of sticks.

2. Take your sticks and climb high into a tree.

3. Draw up a map of where you want to bomb.

4. Look for high-value Communist targets.

5. Once you find your target, lay waste to them until they are a smoking pile of rubble.

6. You only have so many sticks.

14. Stick Size
That's a big stick

1. You might find yourself wondering, How does my stick size compare to other sticks?

2. Is my stick big enough?

3. How big is "big enough"?

4. You can compare sizes with your friends.

5. Having a big stick is not everything.

15. Sticks 101
Back to basics

1. Sticks come from trees.

2. Trees grow just about anywhere.

3. But the biggest and best trees are always in
   the forest.

4. In the forest you are going to find many,
   many sticks.

5. This concludes our lesson for *Sticks 101*.

16. Flip Stick
A game of sticks + flipping

1. Each player gets 2 sticks.

2. One stick is the flip stick, and the other stick is just a stick.

3. Use your flip stick to flip your stick.

4. You can only use your flip stick to flip the non-flip-stick stick.

5. The first player to flip the stick with their flip stick wins *Flip Stick*.

17. Fire Stick
Best played outdoors

1. Go find some sticks.

2. Put the sticks in a pile.

3. Get a can of gasoline and thoroughly douse the sticks.

4. Light a match and off we go.

5. Who knows how to put out a fire?

18. LipStick
I am beautiful

1. Go find a stick.

2. Did you know that many cosmetics are made from plant derivatives (like sticks)?

3. Let's come up with ideas on how we can beautify ourselves with sticks.

4. A stick could be your comb or brush.

5. A stick could also be your back scratcher.

6. I am beautiful.

19. Sticks for Life
I pronounce thee stick and stick

1. Go find 2 sticks.

2. These 2 sticks say they want to get married.

3. As minister, it's your job to figure out if they are compatible.

4. Don't marry them just because you want to get home for supper.

5. Marry the wrong person and you will live your whole life toiling in regret.

20. Whose Stick Is This Anyway?
A game of recall

1. Go find a stick.

2. Go find a friend (who also has a stick).

3. Bury your stick or your friend's stick deep in the ground.

4. Go about your business and return in, say, 6 months or a year.

5. Dig up the stick, and now the fun begins.

6. Whose stick is this—your stick or my stick?

7. How do you really know?

21. Professor Stick
He knows everything

1. Go find a stick.

2. His name is Professor Stick.

3. Professor Stick knows everything.

4. Ask Professor Stick a question.

5. Like "What is the circumference of a circle?"
   or "Why don't really tall buildings fall over?"
   or "How do fish have sexual relations?"

6. Professor Stick knows every answer.

22. Chopsticks
Double the fun

1. Go find a stick.

2. Bend the stick until it breaks.

3. Now you have 2 sticks.

4. *Chopsticks.*

23. Sick Stick
I will save your life

1. Go find a stick.

2. This is your patient, and you must save their life.

3. They may have a cold, typhoid, or the plague.

4. You must diagnose, treat, and console your stick.

5. You're their only hope, or they will surely die.

24. Stickup
Now this could get exciting

1. Put on a big coat.

2. Find a stick that looks like a gun.

3. Put the stick under your coat.

4. Many people will now think that you have a gun on you.

5. This can lead to amusing and unexpected encounters.

6. There's really no telling what might happen.

25. Petrified Stick
Let's learn something new

1. Go find a stick.

2. Could this be a petrified stick?

3. Did you know that petrified wood is a fossil?
   It forms when plant material is buried by
   sediment and protected from decay caused by
   oxygen and organisms.

4. Then groundwater rich in dissolved solids flows
   through the sediment, replacing the original plant
   material with silica, calcite, pyrite, or another
   inorganic material, such as opal.

5. The result is a fossil of the original woody stick
   material that often exhibits preserved details of
   the bark, wood, and cellular structures.

26. Stick Ball
Fun

1. Go find a stick.

2. This is your ball.

3. It doesn't roll, bounce, or do anything like a ball,
   does it?

4. Well, this is the game. This is *Stick Ball*.

5. Play a different game if you don't like it.

27. Stick Clique
Let's make friends

1. Go find several sticks.

2. Become friends with the sticks.

3. Ingratiate yourself with them.

4. Endear yourself to them by offering simple compliments (e.g., "You look nice today") or doing favors for them (e.g., helping them stand up).

5. If they don't include you in their group, that's their choice.

28. Drumstick
Feel the rhythm

1. Go find some sticks and some good-sounding stumps.

2. Now practice, practice, practice.

3. Are you ready to start your own band?

4. *The Ed Sullivan Show* is always looking for fresh new talent.

5. This could be your big break.

6. Do not succumb to drugs, drinking, or general frivolity.

29. Stick Finger
Not really a game

1. Go find some sticks.

2. How many sticks you need depends upon how many fingers you have.

3. Each player uses tape, twine, or baling wire to make their fingers into long, unruly stick fingers.

4. Now pick an everyday activity and see who can do it first.

30. Flystick
The marvel of flight

1. Find a stick that is suited to flight.

2. Players elect how they will bring their stick
   to flight.

3. Options may include throwing your stick, firing
   your stick out of a modified shotgun, or building
   your own trebuchet.

4. *Trebuchet* is a French word for a type of catapult.

5. The trebuchet was used in warfare
   before gunpowder and dates back to
   fourth-century China.

6. A properly built trebuchet will likely be very
   effective in this game.

31. Yardstick
Let's go measure something

1. Go find a long straight stick.

2. Cut your stick down so it is exactly one yard in length.

3. Now try measuring different things with your yardstick.

4. How many yards tall is your uncle Joe?

5. How many yards wide is the town library?

6. Fun.

32. Alfred Stickcock
It's time to make a little magic

1. Go find a stick that has the "wow" factor.

2. As director, you must create a dramatic scene
   and use the stick as your actor.

3. You will want a captivating setting, like a
   battlefield, Mount Rushmore, or a tragedy
   (e.g., the Great Fire), to make your film.

4. The stick will be the hero of the film—you want it
   to suffer and then triumph.

5. Action.

33. Stick Shtick
Haha

1. Go find several sticks.

2. Gather a group of them that will be
   your audience.

3. Use one of the sticks in your comedy routine.

4. You could pretend the stick is an umbrella, a jar
   of pickles, or a long-lost lover.

5. Just because the stick audience doesn't laugh,
   doesn't mean your shtick is no good.

6. This is a tough crowd.

34. Stick Lick
Who knew this could be a game

1. Go find a stick.

2. See how many times you can lick the stick.

3. Maybe see if you can lick all the bark off.

35. Joystick
Life is full of simple pleasures

1. Go find a stick.

2. You say you're not having fun with your stick.

3. Maybe you have the wrong stick.

4. No one said this would be easy.

5. Life isn't always a bowl with cherries.

36. Stick Switch
A new life

1. Go find a stick that looks like you.

2. Switch clothes with the stick.

3. Now the stick will live your life, and you will live
   the stick's life.

4. Check back in, say, 3 months to see if anyone
   has noticed.

37. Stick Together
We will never be apart

1. Get 2 sticks.

2. Put them together.

3. We have a winner.

38. Stick Worth
A game to sharpen your business skills

1. Find a stick that has great appeal.

2. Work up a pitch for your stick.

3. Is your stick really smooth or wet, or does it have a unique smell? Find out what makes your stick marketable.

4. Practice your pitch over and over and over.

5. Find a mark and make your pitch. Don't let them leave until you close the deal.

6. Business.

39. Stick Kaboom!
An exciting game to be played with oncoming railroad trains

1. You'll need 2 players and 2 sticks.

2. Place sticks on railroad tracks.

3. Stand back.

4. Whoever's stick derails a train wins.

5. You may need to go find new sticks.

40. Stick, Pick, Tick, Lick
These are rhymes

1. Get a stick if you want.

2. You don't really need one.

3. The first player says a word that rhymes
   with *stick*.

4. Now player number 2 says a word that rhymes
   with *stick*.

5. Back to first player rhyme *stick,* second player
   rhyme *stick,* etc., etc., etc.

6. Here are a few ideas for the rhymes: Dick,
   Rick, Nick, convict, trick, slick, thick, constrict,
   evict, kick, hick, Bolshevik.

41. Mr. Stick
My new best friend

1. Go find a stick.

2. His name is Mr. Stick.

3. What do you want to do with Mr. Stick?

4. He can do anything you want.

5. He'll do whatever you say.

6. Mr. Stick is really good at floating on his back.

7. Maybe take him down to the pond with you.

42. Sticks and Stones
Not all sayings are really true

1. There's an expression: sticks and stones may break your bones, but words will never hurt you.

2. But is this true?

3. Words can sometimes be hurtful.

4. We need to use our words very, very carefully.

5. And a stick is never going to break one of your bones.

6. That's simply not going to happen.

43. Stick on You
Do you like me?

1. Go find the person you like.

2. Find your best stick.

3. Make sure it's nice and smooth and hard
   and sticky (like a stick).

4. When you see the person you like,
   approach them slowly.

5. When they see you, hand them the stick
   and walk away.

6. Mystery is alluring.

7. Wait.

44. There's No Stick Like Home
We all need a place to call home

1. Get 3 sticks: big stick, medium stick, and small stick.

2. Big stick is your father.

3. Medium stick is your mother.

4. Small stick is your baby brother or sister (you decide).

5. Where would we be without family?

45. Out in the Sticks
Being mean can be fun

1. Grab some friends, some bikes, and a stick and go to the edge of town (where your parents say not to go).

2. Find someone scary looking.

3. Throw your stick at them and say something mean.

4. Now be quick.

5. See how fast you can ride your bike away.

46. Sidekick (Stick)
My best mate

1. Go find a stick.

2. This stick is now your sidekick (stick).

3. Together you can accomplish anything.

47. Stick Stocks
A diversified portfolio allows you to sleep well at night

1. Go find several sticks to start your investment portfolio.

2. If you want to buy a stick, you set a limit order for what price you want to buy it at.

3. If you want to sell a stick, you can sell at market or set a specific target price—it's up to you.

4. Grow your portfolio slowly, carefully.

5. In time you will either get enormously wealthy or lose it all.

48. I'm Stick of You
When it's time to move on

1. If you're tired of your stick, you should get rid
   of it.

2. You could break it into 2 pieces.

3. But now you have double the sticks and double
   the problems.

4. This is quite the predicament you've made
   for yourself.

49. Thick Stick
When a stick is not really a stick

1. Go find a stick.

2. Is it exceedingly thick?

3. That may be a tree.

50. HomeStick
Where would I be without you?

1. Your stick has been with you for a while now.

2. You might think back on simpler times, like when
   you first discovered your stick, and all the great
   joy it has brought to your life since then.

3. Perhaps your family died in the Great Fire.

4. But home is where your stick is.

51. Stick Arithmetic
I am learned

1. Go find a stick.

2. You can use the stick to draw in the dirt and solve
   many mathematical equations.

3. Mathematics is a worthwhile and
   exciting pursuit.

4. People say you can unlock the secrets of the
   world by just drawing equations in the dirt with
   your stick.

52. Polisticks
Like politics but with sticks

1. Go find 2 sticks.

2. These will be your 2 political candidates.

3. Smear one of them for having an affair.

4. Smear the other one for being in bed with the Communists.

5. Neither of these sticks are fit for office.

53. Stick Handler
Are you ready to be a leader of men?

1. Go find a stick that looks menacing.

2. Gather a big crowd. Charge admission.

3. Show the power of the stick to the crowd by
   hitting a home run with it, digging an enormous
   hole, or killing a small animal.

4. The crowd will look at the stick in awe.

5. Now break the stick over your knee.

6. Something so powerful. Broken. You are a god.

7. The crowd goes wild.

54. Matchstick
A game that can literally take a lifetime

1. Go find a stick.

2. Now go find another stick that matches.

3. The new stick must be a *perfect* match to the
   old stick.

55. I'm Love Stick
Love is a many splendid thing

1. Love is said to be one of the best feelings.

2. When you hold your stick, do you feel nervous, happy, and sad all at the same time?

3. Do you feel as though if your stick left you, your life would be devoid of meaning and the room you created in your heart to love your stick would be filled by a bottomless pit of sadness and despair?

4. Love is not for everyone.

56. Stick-Tac-Toe
A twist on the old classic

1. Go find a bunch of sticks.

2. Make a tic-tac-toe board out of your sticks.

3. Use rocks and old railroad spikes for the
   Xs and Os.

4. Best of 3 wins.

57. Game of Sticks
A game from medieval times

1. Gather up a group of sticks.

2. Break up the backyard into different kingdoms.

3. Each stick now must fight to the death!

4. Will the half-blood stick become the ruler of all sticks?

5. It is in the hands of the Lord of Light.

58. The Great Stick Challenge
Does your stick have what it takes?

1. Find 2 sticks that are true competitors.

2. Any stick that is worthy may compete.

3. It's a great honor to compete in *the Great Stick Challenge.*

4. The winner will be determined by an unbiased judge.

5. What the judge says is final.

59. A Stick by Any Other Name
*A game with profound
philosophical implications*

1. Go find a stick.

2. Now give your stick a name.

3. You could name your stick Henrietta
   or Bartholomule.

4. Now ask yourself, If your stick has a name,
   is it still just a stick?

5. Is it your perception that makes something real?

6. What is really real?

60. Stick Fetch
The classic dog and stick game

1. Go find a stick.

2. Go find a dog.

3. Throw the stick for the dog.

4. Explain to the dog how to fetch the stick, return the stick to you, and drop the stick on command.

5. Your dog will derive great satisfaction from this game.

61. Always Be Closing (Stick)
Business

1. There are 3 rules of business.

2. 1. If you don't have it, get it.

3. 2. If you've got it, get rid of it.

4. 3. Always be closing (stick).

62. Why's There a Stick in Your Ear?
When there's nothing better to do

1. Find a small ear-sized stick that you wouldn't mind putting in your ear.

2. Put the stick in your ear.

3. If you walk around town with a stick in your ear, you will be amazed by how many times complete strangers stop you and ask you why you have a stick in your ear.

4. Now that was fun.

63. Stick or Stone
A game that uses your sense of tasting

1. Go find a stick and a stone.

2. Humans only have 5 senses: sight, smell, taste,
   hands, and sound.

3. For this game you will only use your sense
   of taste.

4. Can you figure out which is the stick?

5. What about the stone?

64. Little Stick, Big Stick
David vs. Goliath

1. You will need 2 sticks to play this game.

2. One stick needs to be small and cunning.
   The other stick is big and brutish.

3. Have the sticks compete in various challenges,
   like wrestling, rhetoric, and floating.

4. Competition continues until one stick
   emerges victorious.

65. Stick Trick
Simply amazing

1. Go find a stick.

2. Teach yourself how to do some clever tricks with your stick.

3. How about you break your stick into 2 sticks, set your stick on fire, or make your stick dance a traditional Irish jig.

4. Now take your new tricks to social gatherings, and curry favor with the elite.

66. DipStick
My first real job

1. Go find a long straight stick.

2. Now go around town and offer to check people's oil for them with your DipStick.

3. They may say "I don't have a car" or "Get that stick away from me" or "I'm calling the police."

4. Whatever they say, don't become discouraged.

67. My One True Friend Stick
A friend in need is a friend indeed

1. What makes a true friend?

2. What are the qualities that we look for?

3. A true friend should be loyal (they will never
   contradict you), be trustworthy (they will give
   you money for any reason), and have a mastery
   of the 5 senses (sight, smell, taste, hands,
   and sound).

4. Find a stick with all of these qualities, and you will
   have found a friend for life.

68. Stick-o'-War
A twist on the old classic

1. Go find a very long straight stick (no bark).

2. Divide up into 2 teams.

3. The object of this game is to pull on the stick, dragging the other team through the mud.

4. You can also play by yourself.

5. Find a very long straight stick (no bark) that has a hook on the end.

6. Wrap your hooked stick around a small tree, a fence post, or a stationary railroad car.

7. The object is [*NOTE: what is object? Add later*]

69. The Great Stick Race
A game of endurance and buoyancy

1. Go find some sticks.

2. Now go find some friends.

3. Each player gets a stick.

4. Give yourself first pick to select the clearly superior stick.

5. At the summer solstice players release their sticks into the river.

6. First stick to the ocean wins.

70. Stick Talk
What do sticks really talk about?

1. Find some sticks in their natural state.

2. Do not disturb them.

3. Set up camp and be patient.

4. Observe them from a respectful distance.

5. Listen very carefully.

6. Remember: sticks don't always speak, and when they do, it's very quiet.

71. Rock, Paper, Scissors, Stick
A twist on the old classic

1. Go find a stick.

2. This game plays very similarly to the game Rock, Paper, Scissors.

3. Whoever wins 2 out of 3 games gets the stick.

4. With the stick comes glory, fame, and adulation.

72. Good Stick
A good stick is hard to find

1. Your stick has been very good and deserves to be rewarded.

2. How do we know that your stick has been good?

3. A good stick does what it's told.

4. A good stick does not complain ("I fell to the ground," "I broke in two," etc., etc.).

5. You could get your stick a strawberry milkshake, a Montblanc pen, or a night on the town.

6. Thanks, stick.

73. Short End of the Stick
Such is life

1. The object of this game is to swindle your friends.

2. First, entice your friends to invest in something
   like an ice-cream shop, a real-estate deal, or
   a miracle hair product.

3. When they give you their money, you
   leave town.

4. It's as easy as that.

74. Stick Wars
Defend the stick galaxy

1. Go find a stick.

2. This stick is an estranged orphan child traveling through the galaxy.

3. He is the last of a dying breed dedicated to defending the good side.

4. In order to defend the stick galaxy, he has to kill the leader of the evil side (who is also his father).

5. This stick also dates his sister.

6. Will you choose the dark side?

7. It is time to explore the galaxy and find out.

75. Sticks
A game of high sticks

1. Go find a small stick and a big stick.

2. You are the dealer.

3. Behind your back hold the small stick and the big stick.

4. Everyone places their bets—big stick or little stick.

5. Once bets are placed, you reveal which stick is the winner: big or little.

6. The game of *Sticks* can be played for sticks, comic books, or cash.

7. IOUs are strictly forbidden.

76. Pin the Stick on the Donkey
A twist on the old classic

1. Each player gets a stick.

2. Each player brings their own donkey.

3. If they don't have a donkey, one will be provided for them.

4. Pin your stick to your donkey by using your stick and a sticky substance like sap, caulk, or peanut butter.

5. First to pin wins.

77. Pick of the Stick
I am king

1. Look out into this vast forest before you.

2. All of these sticks are a part of your domain.

3. With a strong will, acute cunning, and ruthless dominance, you will have the pick of the stick for as long as you rule.

4. What will you do with your subjects today?

5. Crush anyone who defies you.

78. Stickology
The scientific study of sticks

1. Employ the scientific method.

2. First, make an observation (sticks are made
   of wood).

3. Second, ask a question (is this stick flammable?).

4. Now make a hypothesis (dousing the stick
   in kerosene and lighting it will start a fire large
   enough to burn down the woods out back).

5. Test your hypothesis. (Yes.)

6. Publish your results.

79. Stick-in-a-Hole
Sticks + holes = game

1. Each player gets 100 sticks.

2. Each player makes a hole.

3. Put your stick in your hole.

4. Bury your stick.

5. Repeat.

6. First one to bury all 100 sticks is the winner.

7. Fun side note: once competition is complete, you can retrieve all buried sticks for a second round of *Stick-in-a-Hole*.

80. Birthday Sticks
The perfect gift

1. How old are you today?

2. Are you 6? You get 6 sticks.

3. Are you 106? You get 106 sticks.

4. You don't want sticks?

5. Who wouldn't want sticks?

6. You are a fool.

81. Kick the Stick
A game of kicking

1. Go find a stick.

2. Now kick the stick.

3. How many kicks does it take to kick the stick to the corner garage?

4. What about to your uncle Joe's place?

5. What about to that old mine shaft that burned down in the Great Fire?

6. Try to better your score on the way back.

7. An official scorekeeper keeps track of the number of kicks by each registered player to each preselected location.

82. Red Stick
Is that stick a Commie?

1. Gather up a group of sticks.

2. One or more of these sticks is believed to be or has been a Communist or a Communist sympathizer.

3. How will you determine which stick is a dirty Commie?

4. Force them to answer your questions.

5. The Communists must be routed out by any and all means necessary.

83. Tag (Stick)
A twist on the old classic

1. Go find the biggest stick you can find.

2. Decide who is going to be "it."

3. The person who is "it" tries to bludgeon the
   other players.

4. If you get bludgeoned, then you are out of
   the game.

5. Make sure to use the heavy, blunt side of the
   stick, not the sharp side.

84. Snow White and the 7 Sticks
Your theatrical debut

1. Go find 7 diminutive sticks.

2. You will play the role of Snow White.

3. You will need a good costume and very
   pale skin.

4. The sticks will play the roles of the dwarfs:
   Grumpy, Dopey, Doc, Happy, Bashful, Sneezy,
   and Sleepy.

5. You may have to carry the show with
   your performance.

85. Stick Names
Who has the best names?

1. Everyone gets a stick.

2. Now set the timer for 60 seconds.

3. Who can come up with the most names for their stick?

4. Not all names are good names for a stick.

5. I once came up with 100 names for a stick in just under 4 hours.

86. I Ride an Old Stick
Howdy

1. Go find a long, spirited stick.

2. Mount your steed.

3. Now go ride into town.

4. Pick up a wanted poster for Bad Johnny Ringo:
   $1,000 for his head.

5. Take a dip of chewin' tobacco.

6. Giddy up, stick—time to hit the ol' dusty trail.

87. Dear Stick
Tell me how you feel

1. Do you take your stick for granted?

2. It's time to stop thinking about yourself all
   the time.

3. Write a letter telling your stick how you feel
   about it.

4. You need to think about your stick's feelings.

5. And you need to communicate better.

6. You can tell your stick "I love you" or "I'm upset
   that you didn't show up to my performance" or
   "I need more physical intimacy."

88. Home-Sweet-Home Stick
Build a house and be a winner

1. First one to build a house out of sticks with a family inside is the winner.

2. Your stick house can be 1 story or 2 stories.

3. Your house can be a traditional colonial or something more modern.

4. You decide where to build your house and how to landscape the surrounding grounds.

5. You do not need to build a carport.

89. Time-Travel Stick
If only we could travel into the future (we can't)

1. Gather a group of sticks together.

2. Place the sticks in a time capsule.

3. Leave other artifacts for the civilizations of the future, like a shoe, some candy, or a sponge.

4. The civilizations of the future will open the capsule and likely remark, "These objects are useless now."

5. They will never understand the simple pleasures of a stick.

90. The Great Stick Council
Your elders know best

1. Gather several large, wise-looking old sticks.

2. These are the members of the Great
   Stick Council.

3. The Great Stick Council will decide on rules like
   speed limits, how many children each citizen can
   have, and curfew.

4. You may not like it, but without the Great Stick
   Council it would be total anarchy.

91. Stick to the Facts
Justice is blind

1. You will need 3 sticks to play this game.

2. One stick is the prosecuting attorney.

3. One stick is the defense attorney.

4. One stick is a low-life drifter.

5. You're the judge.

6. Issue a fair and balanced decision.
   Show no mercy.

92. Stickerella
Does the stick fit?

1. Go find a stick.

2. Only if it's a perfect stick will it fit for the
   Royal Ball.

3. You want to make sure you are looking your best
   with your best stick in hand to impress everyone.

4. Look in the mirror; who is the fairest of them all?

5. Tonight you and your stick will be the talk of the
   Royal Ball.

93. Carrot Stick
Not really a game

1. When people think of a carrot stick, they think of a carrot.

2. That you would eat.

3. But what if you painted a carrot-like stick orange?

4. Then when your friend says they are hungry for a carrot, you produce (from behind your back) your very own carrot stick.

5. Funny.

94. Stick to Stick
This game is not for everyone

1. This is a 2-player, 2-stick game.

2. Players bring their best sticks.

3. There are no rules to the game *Stick to Stick*.

4. You can do whatever you want to
   your opponent.

95. Sticking Point
Has your stick committed insurance fraud?

1. Go find a stick.

2. Now, if that stick has killed a person, defrauded
   an insurance company, or committed arson, that
   would be considered a sticking point to you
   becoming close friends.

3. A sticking point is an obstacle to progress toward
   an agreement or goal.

4. If you've killed someone, this is going to be an
   obstacle to you becoming my close friend.

5. Do not fraternize with a stick such as this.

6. Find a new stick.

96. The Stick Olympics
Let the games begin

1. Everyone brings their very best sticks.

2. Is it winter or summer?

3. This will determine whether you are having the Winter Olympics or Summer Olympics.

4. Ideas for winter events: sliding down an icy surface, hiding in a snowball, etc.

5. Ideas for summer events: floating, "jumping" over high hurdles, etc.

6. Don't let the Russian Commies compete, as they will cheat with performance-enhancing drugs.

97. Stick Search
You should be good at this by now

1. Go find a stick.

2. Did you find a stick?

3. You win.

98. Father Stick
He's a hard man to please

1. Go find a big, fat, mean stick.

2. Say, "Hello, Father Stick. I love you."

3. Then Father Stick might say, "You will never amount to anything."

4. Prove to Father Stick you are worthy by showing him how good you are at doing things.

5. You could float on your back to show him your worth.

6. You may never earn Father Stick's love.

7. But you have to try.

99. Poke a Stick in My Eye
Do you really want me to?

1. Find a sharp, pointy stick.

2. When someone asks someone else to do
   something unpleasant—like take out the trash,
   file their taxes, or go into surgery—they will often
   respond, "I'd rather poke a stick in my eye."

3. When they say this, you simply say "Okay" and
   offer your stick to gouge their eyes.

4. Funny how people don't actually mean what
   they say.

100. Forever Stick
An everlasting stick

1. When we are born, all we have are our 5 senses: sight, smell, taste, hands, and sound.

2. The rest of our worldview is formed by gossip, the opinions of relatives, and traumatic events.

3. But the most important things in life are our memories.

4. When we are lying on our deathbeds, we will ask ourselves, How did I choose to spend my life?

5. Did I raise a family, or did I make a fortune trading oil futures, or did I save a species of monkey from going extinct?

6. Or did I find the joy, satisfaction, and contentment of a stick?

7. A stick that lives not just in my backyard but in my heart forever.

8. A forever stick.